SANTA ANA PUBLIC LIBRARY

AR PTS: 0.5

EXCEPTIONAL AFRICAN AMERICANS

JAY Z

Rapper and Businessman

Joseph Kampff

Enslow Publishing
101 W. 23rd Street
Suite 240
New York, NY 10011
USA

enslow.com

Words to Know

charts—Lists that show how popular a song or an album is.

encore—The last song performed during a concert.

entrepreneur—A person who starts his or her own business.

label—A record company.

lyrics—Words to a song.

projects—A group of apartments or houses built by the government for people who do not have a lot of money.

record deal—A contract to record music.

sample—To use a part of someone else's music in your own music.

studio—A building or room where sound recordings are made.

Contents

Jay Z

CHAPTER 1

School of Hard Knocks

In one of his songs, rapper Jay Z sings about having "99 problems." Being a success is not one of them. Jay Z has made fifteen **studio** albums, and almost all of them have gone to number one on the **charts**. He has owned record companies, a clothing company, and sports bars. And he is married to Beyoncé, one of the most successful female performers ever.

Growing Up in the Projects

Jay Z was born Shawn Carter on December 4, 1969, in Brooklyn, New York. He and his brothers and

CLEANERS

sisters were raised in the Marcy House **projects** in Brooklyn. It was a rough neighborhood. There were lots of problems with drugs and crime. But Jay Z was a happy kid. He liked playing basketball and he did well in school.

Music was very important in the Carter family. Jay Z's parents had a huge record collection. The sounds of soul and funk music often filled Jay Z's home. Jay Z stayed up late banging out beats on his

Life wasn't easy for Jay Z and his family in the early days. Jay Z's mom, seen with him here in 2006, did her best to make ends meet.

kitchen table. He also started writing **lyrics** when he was very young. "If I was crossing a street with my friends and a rhyme came to me, I'd break out my binder . . . and write the rhyme before I crossed the street," Jay Z says.

When Jay Z was eleven, his dad left. Jay Z started spending a lot of time in the streets, where he got the nickname "Jazzy." He started selling drugs. When he was twelve years old, he shot his older brother for trying to steal his jewelry.

Luckily, Jay Z's neighborhood had more than just drugs and crime. It also had hip-hop. Hip-hop is a lifestyle and a kind of music. Jay Z grew up in the center of New York's hip-hop culture. He soon earned a reputation for his rhymes.

Jay Z Says:

"We were living in a tough situation, but my mother managed; she juggled. Sometimes we'd pay the light bill, sometimes we paid the phone, sometimes the gas went off. We weren't starving—we were eating, we were O.K."

CHAPTER 2
From Marcy to Madison Square

Jay Z was one of the best rappers in his neighborhood. In 1989 he got his first chance at making a living from rapping. He went on tour with another rapper from Marcy House projects called Jaz. Jay Z hoped a record company would notice him and give him a **record deal**. When that didn't happen, he went back to selling drugs.

Jay Z finally decided to stop selling drugs after someone shot at him. Jay Z was lucky that he wasn't killed. He knew he had to change his life.

Jay Z decided to start his own record **label**. In 1996 he started Roc-A-Fella Records with two friends.

Hitting It Big

Jay Z released his first album, *Reasonable Doubt*, in 1996. The album sold well and it helped build Jay Z's reputation as a rapper. The hit single from the album, "Ain't No," appeared on the *Nutty Professor* soundtrack. This brought Jay Z's music to a wide audience.

From 1996 to 2003, Jay Z released a new album every year. Almost all of them went to number one on the charts. His biggest hit ever was the single "Hard Knock Life." Jay Z **sampled** the song from the Broadway musical *Annie*. Jay Z's version is the blend of rap and pop music that has made him so popular. In 2003 Jay Z retired from making music.

Once Jay Z found success, he stayed very busy. Here he works in the recording studio on a new album.

Jay Z has won nineteen Grammy Awards for his music. Kanye West is the only rapper who's won more Grammys.

Jay Z Says:

"Everybody likes a story like [*Annie*], when the underdog wins, the orphan gets to live with a rich family. I wanna live with a rich family too. Anybody from a poverty area does—you know, that's a story you can relate to."

CHAPTER 3

Business Man

In one song, Jay Z raps, "I'm not a business man; I'm a business, man." Jay Z is both. In 2004 Jay Z became the head of Def Jam Records. Def Jam is one of the most important labels in hip-hop. Jay Z has been involved in other businesses as well. In 1999 he started a clothing company called Rocawear. When he sold the company in 2007, he made $204 million.

Sports Business

Jay Z has always been interested in sports. He owns a group of sports bars called the 40/40 Club. He has also

Jay Z can often be seen sitting in the front row at NBA games. Here he chats with Kobe Bryant at a Los Angeles Lakers game.

been a part owner of the Brooklyn Nets basketball team. In fact, he helped the Nets move from New Jersey to his hometown of Brooklyn. In 2013 Jay Z started a sports management agency called Roc Nation Sports.

In 2015 Jay Z bought the streaming music company Tidal. With Tidal, Jay Z wants to make

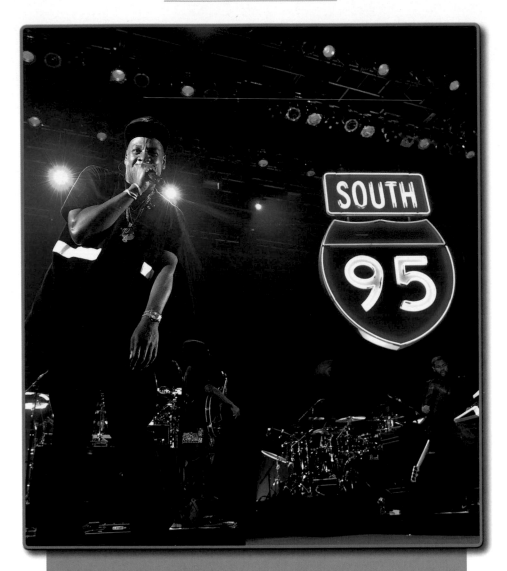

Jay Z performs in a 2015 concert in honor of his new streaming service, Tidal.

sure that the artists who make music are the people earning money from the music. Jay Z has always looked at music as an art form and a business. Jay Z is one of the most successful artists and **entrepreneurs** of all time.

Jay Z Says:

"When I came into the music I was forced to be . . . an entrepreneur. I wanted a deal. I looked everywhere. And when I couldn't get a deal, it was like either quit or, you know, make your own company."

CHAPTER 4

Encore

Jay Z retired from making music in 2003, but he didn't stop rapping for long. In 2005 Jay Z performed his comeback concert. The concert was called "I Declare War." Jay Z invited the rapper Nas onstage to perform an **encore**. Before Jay Z retired, he and Nas didn't get along. After they performed together at the concert, the war was over.

Kingdom Come was Jay Z's first album after coming back from retirement. He has since released four more studio albums. His most recent album, *Magna Carta Holy Grail*, came out in 2013.

In 2010 Jay Z published a book called *Decoded*. In *Decoded*, Jay Z explains how his lyrics relate his life and hip-hop culture. Most of Jay Z's lyrics are inspired by his personal life before he became famous. They are based on his life on the streets of Brooklyn.

Private Life

Jay Z is also a family man. Jay Z married Beyoncé Knowles in 2008. The two have worked on songs

Jay Z signs copies of his book *Decoded* in 2010.

Jay Z Says:

"The whole thing is to learn every day, to get brighter and brighter. That's what this world is about. You look at someone like Gandhi, and he glowed. Martin Luther King glowed. Muhammad Ali glows. I think that's from being bright all the time, and trying to be brighter."

together and also performed together. In 2012 Jay Z and Beyoncé had a baby girl named Blue Ivy Carter. Even though they are two of the most famous people on the planet, Jay Z and Beyoncé like to keep their personal lives private.

Coming from a rough childhood, Jay Z has beaten the odds. As a rapper, businessman, husband, and father, Jay Z is always at the top of the game.

Jay Z and Blue Ivy join Beyoncé onstage in 2014.

Timeline

1969—Jay Z is born Shawn Carter on December 4 in Brooklyn, New York.

Circa 1980—Jay Z's father leaves the family.

1989—Goes on tour with Jaz.

1996—Starts Roc-A-Fella Records and releases his first album, *Reasonable Doubt*.

1998—Releases his bestselling album, *Vol. 2... Hard Knock Life*. The album features the hit single "Hard Knock Life (Ghetto Anthem)."

1999—Founds the clothing line Rocawear.

2003—Retires from making music.

2004—Becomes the president and CEO of Def Jam Records.

2005—Comes out of retirement during "I Declare War" concert.

2008—Marries Beyoncé Knowles.

2010—Publishes *Decoded*.

2012—Blue Ivy Carter is born.

2013—Starts sports agency Roc Nation Sports. Releases *Magna Carta Holy Grail*.

2015—Launches the music streaming service Tidal.

Learn More

Books

Earl, C. F. *Jay-Z*. Broomall, PA: Mason Crest Publisher, 2012.

Gunderson, Jessica. *Jay-Z: Hip-hop Icon*. North Mankato, MN: Capstone Press, 2012.

Nacerous, Roman P. *Jay-Z*. New York: Gareth Stevens Publishing, 2011.

Websites

biography.com/people/jay-z-507696
Includes quick facts, a photo gallery, and quotations from Jay Z.

lifeandtimes.com
Jay Z's website is devoted to art, sports, music, fashion, and culture.

Index

Published in 2016 by Enslow Publishing, LLC.
101 W. 23rd Street, Suite 240, New York, NY 10011

Library of Congress Cataloging-in-Publication Data
Kampff, Joseph.
  Jay Z : rapper and businessman / Joseph Kampff.
    pages cm — (Exceptional African Americans)
  Includes bibliographical references and index.
  Summary: "Describes the life and accomplishments of mogul Jay Z"— Provided by publisher.
  ISBN 978-0-7660-7254-1 (library binding)
  ISBN 978-0-7660-7252-7 (pbk.)
  ISBN 978-0-7660-7253-4 (6-pack)
  1. Jay-Z, 1969—-Juvenile literature. 2. Rap musicians—United States—Biography—Juvenile literature. I. Title.
  ML3930.J38K35 2016
  782.421649092—dc23
  [B]
                    2015029913

Printed in the United States of America

To Our Readers: We have done our best to make sure all website addresses in this book were active and appropriate when we went to press. However, the author and the publisher have no control over and assume no liability for the material available on those websites or on any websites they may link to. Any comments or suggestions can be sent by e-mail to customerservice@enslow.com.

Photo Credits: Throughout book, © Toria/Shutterstock.com (blue background); cover, p. 1 Alberto E. Rodriguez/WireImage/Getty Images; p. 4 Kevin Mazur/Getty Images Entertainment/Getty Images for DirecTV; p.6 Bob Gomel/The LIFE Picture Collection/Getty Images; p. 7 Shareif Ziyadat/FilmMagic/Getty Images; p. 11 Al Pereira/Michael Ochs Archives/getty Images; p. 12 Todd Plitt/Getty Images Entertainment/Getty Images; p. 13 Steve Granitz/WireImages/Getty Images; p. 15 Noel Vasquez/Getty Images Entertainment/Getty Images; p. 16 The Wargo/Getty Images for Live Nation/ Getty Images; p. 19 Eugene Gologursky/WireImage/Getty Images; p. MTV/MTV1415/Getty Images for MTV/Getty Images.